ENGLISH CLUB CREATIVE WRITING JOURNAL VOLUME 1

For Information:
English Club
California State University Channel Islands
1 University Drive
Camarillo, California, 93012
cienglishclub@gmail.com

COPYRIGHT © 2017 by Ethan Powers, Sarah Krashefski, Abigail Ramsey, Mark Westphal, Haylee Chavanne, Nicholas Rada, Sam Diaz

All rights reserved to each author for their own writing, including the right to reproduce their own writing in any form whatsoever.

Editor in Chief: Ethan Powers
Managing Editor: Sarah Krashefski
Copy Editors: Kristen Bromen, Sarah Krashefski, Ethan Powers, Abigail Ramsey
Cover Artist: Gilda Hall

Printed in the United States of America

ISBN-10: 1974529541
ISBN-13: 978-1974529544

Dedicated to the Writers from the English Club Zine Workshop

Table of Contents

Drifting	Ethan Powers	7
The-Man-Upstairs	Sarah Krashefski	25
Rough	Abigail Ramsey	49
Charleston Blues	Mark Westphal	59
Dandelions	Haylee Chavanne	75
Salt	Haylee Chavanne	79
I've Got Wings	Nicholas Rada	83
Archangel	Sam Diaz	91

Drifting

By Ethan Powers

"Drifting! It's drifting fast!" Shouted Patchouli. "Is it safe to catch!?"

Ileu was drifting himself; he was used to the subtle ebb and flow that space exerted on his body.

"You know what we do is never safe Patchouli," hollered Ileu back. "I'll catch it though!"

Patchouli watched from the rim of the ship as Ileu slowly drifted in front of the speeding wreckage hurtling towards him. He calmly put his two arms in front of himself as if he was going to move a boulder, yet it was clear who was going to be pushed. His hands were protected by a pair of extraordinary, skin-tight, spider-silk gloves; his prized possession. He had crafted them himself specifically for this purpose after ten years of gleaning excess silk from a cluster of peculiar spiders he kept on board the ship. Effortlessly, he let the wreckage slam into his outstretched hands as his arms bent at the elbow to absorb the force of the collision. The two objects' strengths tangled as one and Ileu gracefully slowed himself through ever widening circles as the energy dissipated.

"What is it Ileu?" Came down Patchouli's sweet voice.

"It looks like a chunk of a station or maybe some satellites that got tangled up together," he mused. "I'm not really sure what to make of it, but then again I never truly am." He had already worked out his path and was drifting effortlessly towards the ship with the last energy the wreckage had given him. Patchouli, vigilant as always, snapped a picture as Ileu drifted back.

"Hold it up! It looks like some kind of techno-octopus with all those wires dripping off it!" Beamed

Patchouli as she snapped a close up of the object. She preferred a vintage camera to all the ones available now days. There was something endlessly satisfying in the way the Polaroid spits out the moment you just captured. She pinned the Polaroid to the wall as Ileu got aboard and hauled the wreckage to the back of the ship.

"You think you'll be able to use this one Patch? It always looks so torn up to me," he questioned.

Patchouli spoke softly, "All things just need a little understanding and love. If it exists in a physical, material form, than it has something left to offer us."

"I know, Patch. I guess it's just that I'm always impressed with your end of this. I just go out and do the dirty work of catching the dangerous little things. Which is something of a hobby, anyone could do it if they were willing to practice. There's a fleeting feeling of nostalgia; it reminds me of the times I used to go snowboarding on Earth," he replied while loading the wreckage into her converter cube.

Patchouli approached silently as Ileu spoke and rested her arm on his shoulder, "Perhaps you dismiss what you do as impressive because you have memories of a life before this, when people were willing to take risks as you do. I have no purpose without your initial courage and risk. I too have a feeling of nostalgia when I tend to this salvage. It's like pulling a sick little animal from under a house and running home with it; then you show your parents and beg to keep it and promise you'll make it all better."

She reached out and ran her fingers along the lengths of the wires and felt the shape of the wreckage. Ileu had been right on his first guess; it was a piece of a station at one time. It must have been built over three hundred years ago and was drifting for at least a hundred years. She spoke tender words of thanks for all it had done over the years - for the information it stored, for the lives it advanced, and all the work it had put in without so much as knowing its own purpose. The little pile of wreckage cooed and hummed as the dripping mass of wires connected to the converter cube. A pale green glow radiated outward from the cube and illuminated Patchouli's face in front of it. Patchouli gave it the last of what it needed as she leaned in and rubbed her cheek against it saying, "Everything's alright now, there's nothing more for you do to, all is complete, I love you." In response, the little heap of wreckage gave out a delightfully pleasant sigh and disappeared into the converter cube as it flashed a vibrant green. "Thank you," whispered Patchouli as she always did.

"How much did the little techno-octopus leave us?" Cut Ileu's voice through the silence. "It was a cute little one."

"Enough to drift another three weeks. It had quite a build up from about a hundred years of drifting out there." Patchouli had a tear in her eye as Ileu hugged her from behind.

"That's more than the normal release. Your emotions are getting powerful, Patch. I know of a place nearby where we can get some smaller catches and release another couple weeks of energy before drifting out to the deeper reaches again."

"That would be lovely Ileu, will you set the coordinates for us?" Beamed Patchouli. "I'd just love another adventure through the deeps!"

Ileu plotted the coordinates of three areas close in proximity where he was aware of minor wrecks and accidents and let the autopilot do the rest as he returned to Patchouli's side.

"We'll be there in two days, hun. Can I get you a cup of tea?"

****

Patchouli was leaning back in the pilot's seat, which happened to be both the most comfortable seat and best view in the ship. She was gently strumming her small Spanish guitar and singing a sweet, melancholic song. She would occasionally glance down at the display map and smile, even though she was well aware they weren't traveling currently. Something about how the tiny ship was represented on the map compared to space was re-centering and clearing to her thoughts. They had already filled most of their energy supply and this was to be their last stop before maximum capacity.

Ileu entered the room dressed in full suit except for his spider-silk gloves, which he was currently pulling on. He took note of how heavy his footsteps were in contrast to the gentle serenade Patchouli played. He strode in to declare what he always did before jumping, but he froze captivated. He peeled his helmet back and stood there listening to her hauntingly beautiful music, swaying in time. He had never heard her play such a song and listened for a long time without interrupting, until she finished. Then he leaned in and put his arm around her shoulder, nuzzled up to her cheek, and gave her a kiss.

"I'm sorry… I know we have plenty of time for this later once we're in the deeps."

"Patch... that song was beautiful," he said while twirling a bit of her hair in his right hand, "I have the time for your creativity whenever it blossoms."

She turned and looked deep into his eyes and kissed him. "Get out there and catch those little guys so we've got a full charge for the deeps."

He chuckled and said his expected line, "Okay Patch! Time to catch them, watch my back!"

Ileu put his helmet back in place, started running, and jumped out of the ship in the direction of the nearest wreckage. He sailed effortlessly towards it before slowing himself with his boot's reverse boosters. It was an abrupt, awkward jerk for most, but Ileu had learned that if he pulled his legs in towards his chest while engaging the boosters he would do two graceful, backwards summersaults before coming to a stop. These chunks of wreckage were moving at a slow creep making them an easy first catch. He grabbed hold of an edge and engaged the boot's forward boosters just long enough to get him drifting back towards the ship. Ileu firmly believed that any extra time spent saving energy would be paid back more than four times in not having to collect energy again sooner. He planted his feet firmly on the edge of the ship, came to a stop, and handed the wreckage to Patchouli to set aside.

Ileu stuck out his tongue jokingly and said, "You can't catch me!" As he pushed off the ship to get the second chunk of wreckage. Patchouli giggled as he went to collect the second piece in similar fashion to the first and much to her surprise, he was quickly off to gather an unseen third. The third piece of wreckage was tiny, so tiny in fact Ileu had only noticed it drifting while collecting the second piece. As he reached out to take hold of the tiny piece of waste he felt a considerable amount of heat seep into his cold fingers. This wasn't wreckage at all.

"We've got a hot one!" He yelled back to Patchouli.

Patchouli started up in excitement, fumbling to get her own special gloves out from the back of the ship. Ileu was already drifting back toward the ship, his hands perfectly protected from the scorching hot metal.

"Is it a piece we need, Ileu?!" Said Patchouli as she snapped a picture and quickly set the camera aside.

"It looks like it hun, but you're the expert, not me."

Patchouli gently took the glowing piece of metal from him as he reached the ship. She ran giddily with it to the rear of the ship, opened up her far more complicated adapter cube, and placed it inside. She traced intricate patterns across the surface as the heat slowly dissipated. She felt like a child again, lying in a field of grass under the warm summer's sun as the heat then filled her body.

"Little friend, we need you now more than ever. I know you've been struggling to understand your predicament for some time now and are reaching exhaustion. You have so much to give, but nowhere to give it. We can offer you the chance to become part of something larger again if you wish to join us. I promise you won't have to strain like you do now. I can tell you are a highly advanced piece of an engine, and we would love your help."

The tiny piece of advanced technology seemed comforted, letting off more heat before transforming. Like a flower opening, it unfolded from a spherical shape into a flattened circle, humming and buzzing all the while.

"Oh little friend I can see that you accept our offer! You will always be loved and appreciated here!" Stammered out Patchouli as a huge smile came across her face. She rarely got to use the adapter cube, and she loved when she did.

As the little piece of technology fully integrated with the ship, the adapter cube gave off a soft, red light and amplified the humming sound. Ileu swore that the repeated humming sound he heard, "Mm mmmmm mmm mmmmm," was synced to their phrasing of "I love you too." Patchouli claimed she had heard the same when he eventually asked her.

He put his hand on the ship's wall knowing he didn't have Patch's talents and spoke aloud, "Thanks little buddy, I really appreciate you joining us."

Patchouli giggled, "Let's get those two pieces of wreckage into the converter cube, top our energy off, and get out to the deeps! I can't wait anymore! What a day it's been!"

"Aye, aye, captain!" Said Ileu as he winked at her jokingly.

He loaded the pieces one after the other as she appealed to their senses. Both converted to energy for her effortlessly, since she was highly in tune with them after performing an adaptation. Ileu always loved the beautiful colors, green most of all, because they were so inspiring out in space. He often wondered, although he knew the question was unanswerable, if it was the wreckage giving off that light or Patch. He slowly walked to the front of the ship to check the energy levels while Patchouli cleaned up her workspace.

"We've got 98% of our maximum capacity in energy, Patch. I'm setting a course for the deeps. We should be to the outskirts in four days, fully submerged in five." He walked back down the ship, picked up a small blanket as he did, and placed it around Patch's shoulders. He pressed himself against her back and put his arms around her waist, "You must be exhausted, hun. Can I get you a cup of chamomile?"

"That would be lovely dear," replied Patchouli.

The-Man-Upstairs

By Sarah Krashefski

That consistent moment in bed when the smallest sounds taint all comfort of security and amplify the paranoia deep within intuition that compels one to speak up and confront the terribly haunting speculations. The thoughts that analyze *what is reality* unveil the truth within the creation of sound only to impersonate the vibration of what is actually an illusion within one's own physique.

Jane lies awake at night beside her husband Wilbert; consumed with the disturbing noise from upstairs. Abnormal pounding ritually penetrates their ceiling, releasing paint snowflakes to float gracefully onto their bed. Her senses grow immune to the pounding as her eyes close and her thoughts drift to sleep.

Suddenly, the floorboards above their ceiling shift and create an abrupt squeak sound that startles Jane awake; paranoia seeps into her state of mind. She ponders about all the sounds and movements above their apartment ceiling, considering all the normal possible reasons The-Man-Upstairs would be creating such a ruckus. Her thoughts run wild chasing an answer like a dog running after a squirrel—desperately yearning. She persists to ask herself every possible reason for the disturbance, *what could The-Man-Upstairs be doing this late at night, and why didn't the noise wake Wilbert?* Unfortunately, each fantasy she manifests always ends up dark and dreadful. Unless he was moving around furniture or using his floor as a punching bag, there are very few humane causes of this suspicious noise.

Jane looks over to her husband and studies his shadowed face in the dark, wondering *how could he sleep through all this noise?*

"Wilbert, honey, are you awake?" Jane gently whispers.

"Now I am, what's wrong?" Wilbert kept his eyes closed as he turned towards Jane.

"I can't sleep! The-Man-Upstairs is making noise again!" Jane exclaims, surprised that she said exactly what she was thinking.

"What on earth are you talking about?" Wilbert sits up, concerned. Luckily it was dark, and he couldn't see Jane's worried look.

"You didn't hear that?" Jane holds her breath, waiting for Wilbert's response.

"Hear what?" Wilbert looks around for movement, sensing Jane's anxiety.

"Never mind it must have been those damn raccoons." Sweat drips down Jane's neck. She knows the noise didn't stem from petty raccoons. The noise came from upstairs where That-Man resides.

Wilbert shook his head and nudged Jane while shifting his back towards her. At first she wishes Wilbert didn't give up on her initial suspicions so easily, because she knows better than to share her "crazy" ideas with her judgmental husband. She ignores his insensitivity and continues to fantasize about The-Man-Upstairs. She assumes The-Man-Upstairs is not really moving furniture, because he is a MURDERER!

∎∎

The-Man-Upstairs becomes aroused when he inflicts pain on young blonde women. He kidnaps and tortures his blonde playthings for a few days at a time until they are so dismembered that their physical beauty is no longer a defining attribute. According to Jane's TV show "Criminal Minds," a sexual release when imposing physical agony defines a sexual sadist.

When The-Man-Upstairs reaches his terminal point with each woman, he disposes their bodies in the cold wet earth near a field populated with lilies parallel to a hiking trail a few miles away; where he buried his first victim—his wife.

Upstairs a twenty-three-year-old woman named Marina, who The-Man-Upstairs snatched twenty-four hours ago, was stashed away for her first play-date. Marina awoke from a few hours' sleep after pounding the enclosed closet walls and screaming most the night. She studies the light creeping from under the door as it slowly disappears. Her breathing starts to escalate as she hears the front door open. Confusing images of a cold rustic van from the kidnapping fill her subconscious. For a quick second, Marina forgets she is bound to a computer chair, and as she struggles to move, her skin from her wrists peels off like the outside of an orange peel. The fear of her unknown kidnapper produced enough adrenaline for her to withstand the pain from the huge gash that bruised her skull. She assumes her attacker crept up behind her and hit her over the head when she was on her night run.

    The-Man-Upstairs gently places his car keys on the counter and begins his end of work ritual. He takes his black recently polished dress-shoes off and walks them into his wardrobe. He had a great day at the office, reminiscing about his new plaything he stowed away in his hallway closet—excited to play with her later. He replays the time he spent with his previous playthings in his torture room; wondering if Marina is a screamer too. He imagines it like a video replaying over and over again in his head.

He walks towards the spare-bedroom passing the hallway closet with an intimidating grin. His so called "spare-bedroom" is actually a torture room where he hangs his playthings from a heavy-duty hook bolted to the ceiling. The whole room is blinding-white with a shiny metal table in the corner, next to a series of cabinets constructed above a sink. The florescent lights capture every inch of the room—spotless like a hospital. The-Man-Upstairs glides across the black tiled floor with his socks, and starts to prepare for the bloody night ahead. Every single movement of his preparations is carefully planned and determined through decades of practice. He covered the torture room with plastic, and places each of his surgical tools half an inch apart on the metal table. As he finishes his preparations, he presses play on the portable stereo sitting on the counter by the sink. He can no longer conceal his excitement as he ties a bow behind his back to secure his butcher apron—a smirk escapes from his mouth. Classical music consumes the whole room as he hums on his way towards the hallway.

The-Man-Upstairs opens the hallway closet door, as a muffled scream escaped from Marina's duck taped mouth. He pushes the back of the computer chair as she tries to escape the pounds of duck-tape around her waist, chest, and legs. Her violent wiggling was no use as she enters the prepared torture room. His smile extends from ear-to-ear as he rubs his hands together while staring at Marina with lust—severely violent intentions.

The smell of freshly laid plastic awakens a child inside of The-Man-Upstairs; thrilled like waiting in line for his favorite rollercoaster. He secures himself inside his rollercoaster's seat as he carefully puts on his mask and gloves. Marina's desperate screams arouse The-Man-Upstairs as he cuts deep into her flesh. The color red coats his blade like spreading strawberry jam across toast in the morning. His climax was at the top of his rollercoaster as he was about to fall straight down the dip. Marina cries and wishes all the pain and torture is a dream. Her screams lessened into whimpers and cries, after hours of blade in flesh penetration. Once Marina passes out from her worst nightmare, The-Man-Upstairs plateaus and begins to clean up the bloody mess.

    He un-hooks her from the ceiling and binds her back to the computer chair. After wheeling her to the hallway closet, he stood in front of her for a minute. As he wipes blood from her face and runs his fingers through her soft blonde hair, he whispers, "I'll see you tomorrow, my beautiful doll."

∎∎

Downstairs, Jane and Wilbert get ready for their day. Jane is in the shower trying to wake up from her sleepless night as Wilbert sits at the kitchen table with his coffee and newspaper. Jane is still obsessed with the constant noise The-Man-Upstairs makes late at night. After she gets out of the shower, she contemplates how to convince Wilbert to help her investigate what's really going on upstairs.

She plops down in her chair at the round kitchen table, staring firmly at Wilbert to get his attention.

"Hi honey. I left the coffee pot on for you," Wilbert said while continuing to read his paper. Jane's face displays frustration as she almost glares a hole straight through his newspaper. Wilbert turns the page, and an article with the headline "The 'Slicing-Master' Strikes Again," catches Jane's observance.

"Wilbert, did you read the article about the 'Slicing-Master'?" She asks with curiosity as Wilbert flips the newspaper to recall the article.

"Yes, I did. It was very disturbing. Poor woman in her early twenties was tortured and killed. A group of hikers found her body in the forest a few miles away from here. Looks like the killer didn't dig a big enough grave for her, because the rain washed out most of the surrounding dirt." Wilbert informed like a news reporter. Jane had a look on her face like she saw a ghost, well in this case heard about a ghost. She shifts in her seat, and begins to speak.

"Wilbert, I know you're going to think I'm paranoid, but just listen. What if this 'Slicing-Master' killer is The-Man-Upstairs?" Jane waits anxiously for his response.

"Honey, maybe your limited sleep time is affecting your condition. Are you taking your medication?" Wilbert asked while looking at her with concern. Jane is annoyed, frustrated, defensive, and most of all disappointed her husband is not taking her seriously.

"Seriously Wilbert? Of course, I'm taking my fucking meds!" Jane felt the anger floating up her throat like a toxic gas. "Can you please keep an open-mind for once in your life, and consider my idea." Jane takes a deep breath while trying not to raise her voice. Wilbert concentrates for a moment on what he was about to say.

"I should call Doctor Johnson." Wilbert whispers to himself, forgetting Jane was right in front of him.

Jane rises from her seat and slams her palms against the kitchen table making a loud thud. She glares at Wilbert with rage as the sight of a red background encloses her vision of him. "Why Wilbert?" Jane breathes heavily as Wilbert was silent. "Because you think I'm crazy? Huh?" The veins around her neck bulged as she steps away from the table and starts to pace back and forth.

Wilbert gets up and follows her. "Jane, please. I really think we should include Doctor Johnson on this." He pleads as he tries to grab her hand, but she pushes him away.

"Fuck off Wilbert. I don't need you or a doctor." Jane yells as she runs out the back door. She unlocks the car door. "I'm right. I know I'm right." She turns the ignition on and backs out of the driveway. "You'll see," she said to herself with hope.

■■

The rain pours onto Jane's beat up powder-blue Volkswagen as she parks parallel to her neighborhood's nearby police station. Sitting for more than a few minutes, Jane focuses her attention more on the filtration of citizens and police officers going in and out of the building, instead of planning what to say when she walks inside. Jane could not help but think, *What if they don't believe me? What if they think I'm crazy too?*

Jane quickly grabs her purse and keys, bolting out of her car before she can change her mind otherwise. Left foot, right foot, step, step. Jane is consumed with the anticipation, avoiding eye contact along the steps by police officers suited in rain gear and Glock pistols holstered to their hips.

As she finally enters the police station, she looks around to see where the appropriate place would be to talk to someone. She walks up to a glass window with a large Caucasian female officer typing vigorously. The policewoman swings her seat to face Jane.

"How can I help you?" The policewoman asks, as she looks Jane up and down. Jane shifts her footing from left to right.

"I was wondering if I could talk to someone concerning the 'Slicing-Master' investigation." Jane timidly said. The policewoman gets up from her raised computer chair.

"I'll be right back, let me get someone."

Jane sits down at the nearest seat next to the window and waits. She notices her hands shaking uncontrollably. She quickly pulls her black sweater sleeves down and shoves her hands in her pockets.

Jane hears the door behind her open swiftly. A man in a white dress shirt, blue tie, and gray pants, walks in her direction.

"Hi, my name is Detective Wilson. Officer Mills claimed you are inquiring about the 'Slicing-Master'?" He said with his hand already shaking Jane's.

"Uhh, yes. That's right." Jane releases while clearing her throat.

"Come with me." Jane follows Detective Wilson back through the door he came from, towards a large room with various desks.

"Please, have a seat." Detective Wilson holds his hand out towards a chair next to a desk with his name displayed. Jane sits down as per his request and crosses her arms around her faded brown satchel purse. He opens a large file at his desk. His face embodies a transparent look of empathy as he guides his glasses to his face. Even after studying the "Slicing-Master's" file for months, he still couldn't hide the initial reaction of sorrow for the mutilated women that are described and photographed.

"So, what can you tell me?" Detective Wilson questions after taking a deep breath. He sets the file down and waits for Jane's intel. She notices three inches of a photo sticking out of the file showing strands of bloody blonde hair covered in mud.

He clears his throat, and Jane quickly looks up from her analysis of the horrific portion of the photo.

"I believe The-Man-Upstairs from my apartment is the 'Slicing-Master' from the article I read this morning in the newspaper." Jane blurts out, hoping for the best. Detective Wilson's bushy black eye brows move closer together creating a crease in between.

"How do you know he's the murderer?" Detective Wilson was unconvinced.

"I hear strange violent noises in the middle of the night through my ceiling. It's just not normal. I'm concerned." Jane elaborated. Detective Wilson stays quiet for a moment, contemplating how to direct this accusation of hers.

"Okay, we'll check it out for you, but I'm going to need your address. May I see your driver's license?" Detective Wilson persisted and starts typing on his computer. Jane reaches for her wallet and pulls out her driver's license suspiciously.

"Here you go." She placed the license on the desk. Detective Wilson snatches it and starts entering in her information into his database.

"Great. I'll get this back to you, but would you mind waiting in the lobby for me?" He signals for an officer to escort her to the door.

"Sure. Thank you for your time." Jane says hesitantly while on her way out.

■■

After an hour of waiting in the police station lobby Jane receives her driver's license back and is sent home to wait some more. She couldn't help but notice Detective Wilson's attitude changed when he came back to the lobby—cold and vague about his next steps on bringing The-Man-Upstairs in for questioning. Jane wonders what information he found when he searched her name, and how her previous stay at the psychiatric hospital was documented in correlation.

Thankfully Wilbert was at work and out of Jane's mind. She nervously sits by her charging phone and stares out her apartment's wide front window.

The sky turned black and the moon shined bright. Jane ritually peeled back her blinds to see if the police were coming to search the upstairs apartment, but nothing—no one came.

■■■

Wilbert gently breathes through his nose as Jane lay awake anxious—waiting for the slightest movement from upstairs.

Expected footsteps crept from upstairs, followed by two large bangs that rattle the wall behind Jane's head. Gripping her sheets, she throws them off with one single motion and marches out the front door with only a gray cotton nightgown swaying from the sides of her thighs. The moist night wind pushes her back as she ventures up the eerie stairs while holding her husband's baseball bat by the middle of the barrel. The hair on her arms and legs stick straight up as she releases a shiver from the cold—maybe her anxiety—or both.

When Jane reaches the top, she knocks on the upstairs door with force. She feels the escaped vibration from her knock transfer to the floor under her. She remains two feet behind the door—waiting. After a minute, Jane suspiciously looks through the filthy side window. There are no lights on and little to no furniture in sight. The apartment looks abandoned and forgotten. She stands there another few minutes hoping for an answer, but nothing. As she makes her way down the stairs defeated, the wind blows abruptly behind her to reveal an eviction notice beside the planter.

Rough

By Abigail Ramsey

Every morning is just the same. The alarm blares, creating uncomfortable echoes in your eardrums. You become hyperaware of how dry your mouth is from the night before, yet you still hit the snooze button seven times. You finally roll out of bed because the urge to piss is overwhelming. Before tucking your phone in your sweatpants, you check the time – 6:08 a.m.

You make your way through the maze of scratchy carpet, dirty clothes, and shoes over to the bathroom. Your feet touch the frozen tile floor of the bathroom causing your entire body to tense up. You turn on the light, which sends a sharp pain to the back of your eyes. You squint and get dizzy, but you manage to find the toilet seat and crack it open. You press your eyes shut to protect them from the imposing light. After what felt like a lifetime spent over the toilet, you finish up and find your way out of the frozen bathroom. You step back onto the scratchy carpet that spreads from the living room to the kitchen. The lights are all off, and your eyes still hold the remnants of light from the bathroom, not allowing you to adjust to the black abyss ahead of you. Despite your carefully calculated steps, you still trip over the shoes you took off in the middle of the floor when you got home late last night.

    You finally make it into the kitchen with even more frozen tile. You flick the switch on the wall to your right; the lights turn on, but they are oddly dim as one of them flickers. Everything in your apartment seems to be wearing away. The sound of the refrigerator whirs in the background. The faucet releases one drip of water every two seconds like an ancient torture device. The paint on the walls may have been a bright white back in the day. Now, it is just a cringe-worthy yellow, as if a layer of smoke has rested itself on every inch of the walls. You make your way to the counter with the tile that is grasping for its life on the grout that has forgotten its purpose. You reach for the coffee beans, and instantly the fog that was looming over you seems to lift from your mind. They say people feel that way in the company of someone they love, but you have never encountered someone who does that. Only coffee. You pour the beans into the grinder. You do not need to measure anymore because you have memorized the accidental line in the grinder that happens to create a perfect, strong, rich cup of coffee. It's an art form really; if there is one thing you are good at, it's making a cup of coffee. You walk away as the automatic grinder cracks through the beans, sending the rich aroma throughout the kitchen. In that moment, mornings do not seem to be so rough.

You grab the carafe and head for the ancient torture device of a sink to fill up the pot with four cups of water. You rest your hand on the counter as the water flows, but in your drowsiness your hand slips on the broken tiles. Three shards of a cobalt blue tile clink towards the bottom of the sink. You turn off the water, collect the tiles, and follow a small pool of dark red blood on the edge of the sink. Not amused, you pull the palm of your hand up to eye level to see a steady flow of blood pooling right beneath your thumb. *So much for mornings not being rough*, you think. You grab the closest dishtowel and tightly wrap it around your hand. You fail to remember the last time you washed that towel – two weeks at least.

More frustrated than ever, you return to the one thing that can make you happy. You switch off the grinder and pour the grounds into the patient filter. It sounds like sand going through an hourglass, counting down the seconds until you will hold perfection in your hands. You press the start button waiting for the first hiss of the water to heat up. But something's wrong. Panic ensues. Not even lights are flashing. You check the power cord – plugged in. The fog bears down on your mind again. You pinch the bridge of your nose between your eyes. You press the start button one more time while praying to the God you don't believe exists. Still nothing. In a fit of rage and fear of abandonment you begin hitting the coffee maker, forgetting the sting of the cut in your hand – flesh and dishtowel clapping against cheap plastic - but still no response. With your hands perched on the counter top and a deep sigh, you accept defeat.

You move out of the kitchen, tripping on the same pair of shoes as before. Without thinking, you pick up one of the shoe culprits and hurl it further into the black abyss of the living room. There is a thud as it hits the hollowed wall across the room. You move towards your bedroom, pulling your phone out of your sweatpants pocket. The dishtowel around your hand causes you to fumble trying to enter the passcode. You go to Messages and begin tapping away a convincing text to your boss.

> *"I won't be able to make it in today. Came down with something over the weekend. Plan to make a doctor's trip. Hopefully see you tomorrow."*

You look it over real fast, proud of yourself, and hit send – 6:20 a.m. You turn your phone off, fold the blankets back in bed, and bury yourself underneath. The blankets brush against your arms and bare feet. *It's only Monday,* you think as you rest your head back on your pillow. Within seconds you feel your eyelids becoming heavy as if elephants were laying on them. You drift back to sleep to dream about how an elephant might feel with its rough skin being enveloped in blankets.

Charleston Blues

By Mark Westphal

My name is Joshua Wendell Garrett, but most people call me Josh. I am twenty-three years old. I started attending the College of Charleston last year when I moved away from my parents in New Jersey. I can't imagine why I moved down to South Carolina other than it was far away, and it was not Florida. I brought with me all the money, music, and clothes I possessed. I felt as though I needed nothing else.

I was extraordinarily lucky to land a job and an apartment in the first couple of weeks. I worked my first year in college as a cook in an oyster bar, which was not a great job to say the least. I hated my boss. I hated the horrible music my coworkers played in the kitchen. I had a rivalry with some shit-head sous chef named Jackie over god knows what. I also worked full time while school kept getting more intense. My contempt for work came to the surface more often; especially when my boss got in my face one day for not coming in on my day off to cover some lazy fuck who didn't show up, I nearly lost my temper. But in the end, all I did was nod my head and say I was sorry and list off excuses—I had a lot of homework that day, I didn't get his call, etcetera, etcetera, etcetera. It was my go to answers for avoiding work.

During my first semester of school, I made it my goal to have sex with one of the fine southern ladies at my school. It's amazing how much better the girls look in a different town. When I was about a third of the way into the semester I grew tired of attending Christian functions, ice cream socials, and the biology club. All of which didn't include a single girl who wasn't already spoken for. My strategy wasn't working. I decided to give rumors a chance.

There was this girl I heard about named Tiffany, and she was supposed to be the biggest s. campus. Upon hearing this bit of rumored information in a Chick-Fil-A, I was way too ecstatic. Had I gotten so desperate? Probably. It didn't bother me at the time, and it still doesn't bother me now. I hoped to God to run into her. If what I was hearing about her was true, and she would fuck just about anyone, then I might have a chance.

I got my wish just one day later. Apparently, she was in one of my classes all along and I never noticed her! What was even more stupid was that she sat only two seats away from me. I remember seeing her for the first time. She was smiling and laughing at a nearby conversation, and I remember thinking she was very beautiful. No wonder it seemed easy for so many dudes to go down on her. After class got out, I made an effort to go talk to her. Our teacher made us form study partners for the test next week, and when I noticed everyone left the room around her, I thought it was my ultimate opportunity to get with her.

"Hey."

She didn't hear me at first, but I tried again, this time with an agenda encouraged by our professor: "Excuse me, but do you need a study partner? I don't have one yet and I'm not very prepared for the midterm."

Then she heard me, and turned to face me. "Oh, ummm me neither," she paused, "Sure. I'll be your partner. What's your number?"

I gave her my name, then my number.

"I'm Tiffany," she says to me cheerfully, "But most guys call me by my middle name, Janet."

"Janet huh?" I said with disgust. I don't like that name, "Can I just call you Tiffany?"

That took her off guard. I don't know why I said that. "Okay, whatever works for you!" She says in her still cheerful voice, "When did you want to meet?"

"Saturday work?"

"Yeah! Where?"

"Well that depends. Do you like seafood?"

***

I didn't take her to my restaurant; I took her to another oyster bar. $3 Happy hour oyster shots, $5 champagne oysters, and with every two orders of oysters you get a free vodka gimlet. Good shit. I am an oyster fiend, after all. I guess I can thank my parents for that.

When we got to the bar we sat down and I got two orders of oysters to get my free gimlet. As soon as

I told her about the happy hour special, she was so excited that she took my gimlet as soon as it got to the table.

"Wow Josh," she started, "I've never had a 'study session' so …. gourmet."

"Well, only the best for my new study partner," I replied, "Now, I'd like to talk about school stuff for a while."

"Oh, yeah about that," she said, "I totally forgot to bring my notes."

"Ha! Me too! How stupid of me!" We both laughed. "But for real, though, that test is gonna be easy as fuck, amirite?"

"Yep. Way too easy, makes me wonder why the teacher made us form study groups in the first place." She said before downing the rest of the cocktail.

We hit it off exceptionally well, too well. She talked about her favorite classes and what she was going to school for, Biochemistry. She seemed to really like Biochemistry, because she freely talked about how much she knew about molecular biology components. This was the kind of thing that made me almost hate biology, but I found the way she talked about it fascinating for some reason. I started talking about how I was new to the school, how I love sea animals enough to be a marine biology major.

"Well if that's the case, why're you in Charleston and not still in New Jersey?" She asked.

"Don't like it there anymore." I said truthfully.

"Why not? *I* like New Jersey. If I were you I would have stayed there."

"I felt trapped, I guess. My life wasn't as interesting there."

"Oh," she pondered, "Bad past? Family issues?"

"No," I paused, "I guess I'd describe it as a whole lot of nothing."

She stared into my eyes as I finished saying that, and I felt still. It was a brand-new feeling; I was almost shocked, surprised. I'm not big on eye contact, so it did make me uncomfortable, but at the same time I felt we were making a connection beyond the conversation, beyond the fact that I found her physically attractive, beyond our names and who we were. When I was looking in her pale green eyes that I saw something that I never saw before. I knew in that moment she was into me. It was a dead giveaway. We all know that when a man and a woman make eye contact for longer than a minute, it's because they were forced by some particular social circumstance. In this case it was because we wanted each other.

I blinked and took a bite out of a now-cooled-down oyster: "So how long have you lived here?"

Her answer was delayed: "In Charleston?"

I nodded.

"Five years. I moved here from Columbia. I wasn't getting along with my dad and I liked it here much better anyways."

"I see," I noticed the place we were at was starting to get packed, so I changed the subject: "You wanna come back to my place? It's starting to get loud in here."

"Sure." She said almost without hesitation.

***

We got to my apartment. Thankfully, I had enough money and luck to get one where I lived alone.

Another good thing too: it wasn't one of those horrible fucking historic buildings that made Charleston look like it is stuck in the 19th Century. This meant I was not only in a building that was a rarity in a historic city, but it also meant that I was paying rent that included good plumbing, air conditioning, and heating. Not that you would need a heater in Charleston; it was so fucking humid 24/7 that going outside meant covering oneself in a thin layer of Earth's sweaty gym sock.

My place was fairly simple; a kitchen with a range, plenty of cabinet space, a table comfortable enough for two but enough room for a third wheel, one bathroom, one bedroom with a queen bed and a small rectangular closet. There's no decorations on the walls except for my bedroom, which was plastered with posters of my favorite bands; Nirvana, The Foo

Fighters, Rage Against the Machine, a signed Reel Big Fish tour poster I got when I went to see them, The Red Hot Chili Peppers, a signed poster from Less than Jake, and one Disturbed poster my friend gave me as a parting gift before I moved away. I don't even like the band but I like my friend, no matter how far away he is.

I showed Tiffany in like the true gentleman I tried to be.

"Not bad," she said, "Not bad at all."

"Thanks. Rent's pretty high though, but hey; it works for me."

She asked me if I have anything to drink. I told her I was saving some local brew in case someone came over. I got myself one too and we sat down at my comfortable table. I staved off my urge to tell her she was the first person to come over. I wanted to tell her she was beautiful, sexy, kind, fair, and everything I wanted in a woman—but I did not. Instead, I stayed quiet for a few brief moments before I broke the silence.

"Do you feel comfortable?"

"With the chair or with you?"

I shrugged and said: "Both, I guess."

"Huh...Well, I guess I feel pretty good."

I grinned and nodded. Our eyes met again. It was like the restaurant again, except quiet and more intimate. The blues play in my head, like hearing "Layla" by Derek and the Dominoes over the speakers at the restaurant. I don't want to look away this time. This time I didn't see someone who would fuck just about anyone; I saw someone who just might have found me attractive enough to look beyond my eyes and deeper into my bullshit. She knew who I was, and it made my blood as blue as Clapton's singing.

"Yeah, actually, I feel very, very comfortable," Tiffany said, chuckling tenderly.

My right-hand moved across the table, and she grabbed it. Her grip on my hand was tender, loving. I intensified my grip on her hand, and she reciprocated. The look in her eyes became more tender, and I began to feel the urge to move closer to her. She was so beautiful, yet so down to earth. How could I not love her? Was I being manipulated? I didn't know. Maybe I'm too much of an open book, like a rulebook to an easy board game. Once she figured out the rules, she started to play my game and win.

"Wanna cuddle?" She said with her smile disappearing into a serious demeanor.

Cuddle?! I thought it was a good start at least. I told her my bed was the most comfortable place to do that. We finished our drinks and moved to the bedroom. As soon as she lay down, I asked if she would like to listen to some music. She said yes. I put on my favorite album and then I lay down beside her. She said my taste in music is unique, and I told her that being unique is what I aim for. She laid her head on my shoulder and breathed slowly.

"Don't get up. I'm more comfortable here than ever." She breathed before falling asleep.

Dandelions

By Haylee Chavanne

I'd plant you as dandelion seeds if I could.
Weeds were always beautiful to me

raising themselves, willful, from
this crass earth.

Grow,
                regardless of when I leave you.

I cannot stem your fear forever –
time will never be your certainty.

Dandelions grow,
ignorant to our constructed
tomorrows and yesterdays.

See their petals,
how gladly they catch the
                        light –

        I'll solemnly plant you beside them,

and a woman
who has never learned a prayer
        will whisper your name into the earth

            as though she always knew.

Salt

By Haylee Chavanne

Why have the gods lied to us –
tonight, while the sea is no giver of life but
blue ether
distilled,
fragments of unwashed fancy.

I kneel on those shores to scoop
the ancient salt in these hands –
trembling, childlike, crawling
slurping in the tide.
A hundred thousand years and more condensed
into an iota.

The moon is a hanging fruit and dips low
into the shore. The sea,
the ether, burns the air even as it
lures us
with sweet scents and mirages. I
will pluck the fruit,
now rotting,

puncture it with a
bite, hope for at last,
a resting heartbeat – gain only
intoxication –I try
to walk backwards into something
I never was –
a grain of salt
in the unending sea.

I've Got Wings

By Nicholas Rada

Victor Nelçe had never been to this particular eatery before. He did his best not to frequent any establishment out of fear of familiarity, and the namelessness he found was about all he could to do find an appetite. This location seemed fine. It had a rather offbeat vibe, being in a small town outside of a big city. He decided that most of the few faces here were from out of town. They were probably driving through like himself. Nelçe had planned on stopping by for only a short while—this stop being the only deliberate decision in his drive. After absently approaching the counter, Nelçe was, to say the least, exasperated to find himself face to back with the familiar form of a man who held a good deal of significance in the reasoning behind his drive this morning. The anticipated interaction morphed a conflicted expression onto Nelçe's face, but the difficulty lied in where his disappointment was being placed—the weak smile or the soft eyes. It didn't really matter. By this point the reaction had become a habit, and the man never seemed to notice so Nelçe stopped noticing as well. At least that is what he would tell himself.

"Oh hey, Vic, what's up?" the man said.

"Hey, not much. I'm just grabbing a bite to eat." Nelçe said.

He tried to ignore the man and scanned over the menu above. Being shorter than the man—who was tall in comparison to Nelçe even with himself being a respectable height—it was difficult for Nelçe not to shift focus back to him.

"What are you doing out here?" the man asked.

"I went for a drive and decided to get something to eat." Nelçe repeated.

"Yer not stalking me, are ya? Nyuh-haha."

"No."

"Hey, I'm just kidding," said the man. "Do you wanna eat together?"

"Sure."

They sat down at a relatively centered, windowed booth, Nelçe could not help to notice the spaciousness. It was suffocating. He excused himself to the restroom, forestalling conversation for as long as he could help to, but the inward dialogue wasn't too favorable of a supplement. He could just leave, but his character wouldn't appreciate the rudeness. He could lay out his feelings to the man, but he had the impression it would do more harm than good. He could just stay in the restroom for the rest of the day and hope for the man to leave. Of course, whatever he could do would just provide fuel to a fire Nelçe hadn't started but had to deal with. And, of course, Nelçe had stopped caring about dealing with the fire. At least that is what he would tell himself.

Nelçe never used the restroom for its intended purposes.

Returning in more or less the same state, Nelçe sat down across from the man.

"It's pretty funny running into you here," the man said.

"Yup."

"So, uh, I was meaning to text you later. A couple buddies of mine and I are going camping tonight close by."

"Oh, where?"

"Some place off a trail West in the mountains. It's kind of impromptu, but you should come."

Nelçe looked at the server bringing their food. "Sure, I'm not doing anything."

"Cool. I'll let the others know."

"Cool."

The server placed their food down, and they exchanged the appropriate pleasantries. They ate in what Nelçe thought the man thought was an awkward silence.

"Hey, you sure you want to come? Everything okay?" The man asked.

Nelçe gave him a smile that he thought was enough. "Yeah, of course. I'm for it."

It was enough.

Later in the evening, Nelçe arrived at the trailhead half expecting to see no one and half wanting to see no one. He wasn't sure how those sentiments translated when he did, but he didn't think about it too much. For whatever good it meant, Nelçe kept a sleeping bag in the trunk of his car because you never know, so he felt more or less prepared for whatever the trip entailed.

Archangel

By Sam Diaz

Gunfire, each shot like a crack on a singular black surface. Bolts of golden light revealed dust, glass, and the remains of what used to be a house's wall. The sidewalk shone with millions of shattered window pieces. The car gunned its engine and thundered down the road, leaving sick clouds of dirt in its wake. A door across the street slammed open, the number for the police already dialed, as he sprinted across the street towards the house.

Breaking down the door, he nearly vomited as he saw the shredded corpse on the ground. Like the street, the inside of the house was peppered with glass. Crimson pools floated on a snow-white couch. Bloody glass shards led towards a doorway. He called out hoping someone could hear him. He tripped on the coffee table and a loud crash was the result. Regaining his balance, he followed the drops of blood to an open back door and a broken fence. Standing in the doorway, the Witness' chest heaved. He waited, desperately wondering what the hell was going on.

Ten Years Later

Nothing is worse than a feeling of isolation. Surrounded by dozens of warm bodies, personalities, individuals with countless stories and emotions...the canorous din of humanity silenced. It was like a blindness, walking through city streets, looking at everything but unable to see. It was imprisonment in the shadows of one's own body, bearing the demons without listening to the songs of the angels.

Staring at the blank page before her, Sadie was confronted with the same conundrum she had faced countless times before. How does someone write without having lived? Undoubtedly the bottle of scotch James had offered would help, but then what? Drown in alcohol to flood her mind with answers? He may not have understood her forced abstinence from alcohol, but it didn't matter. Drunk or sober, she would still be faced with the Question. Staring at the blank page allowed her to ignore the disgusting black rain that fell from the sky outside her window. The smog filled air had blown in from across the Atlantic, vomiting its poison across Brooklyn Harbor.

    Sadie found herself outside with her hood up, and her hands in her pockets. The black rain ran thick like sludge down her shoulders. Little black rivers traced their way mockingly towards the concrete beneath her feet. She walked across cracked streets and abandoned apartments, all while the face of President Samson smiled down on her like a proud god. She had defaced the billboard countless times, but destroying Ethan Samson's face did nothing to help her. It did nothing to make her forget.

One sterling silver needle, empty of its golden fuel. Her father's head resting against the pillow, his breathing halted. She screamed for him, his white hair pressed to his head by the sweat that just moments ago had signaled his desperate clutch on life. The needle sat on the table where it had been left, empty of the poison that it had just administered.

Pushing open the door to an idle diner near the roiling ocean, she sat in a booth far from the languid crowds that frequented the diner. Again she was pulled from her musings to look at the sole partner she had.

The man was unusually pale, his eyes trained on the ground or the menu in front of him. He was from New Coast, rumors abounded that he had once been a family man who had seen something he shouldn't have. All Sadie knew was that he was always at the bleak diner staring at his menu. The way he stared at it reminded Sadie of how she must have been staring at that blank page. He was waiting to talk, to share his story. He wanted to add to the clamor of humanity around him.

Sadie stood and fought against the tides of fear. She trekked across to his table and sat across from him, knowing that the story he held behind his eyes could free hers. He raised his eyes to look into hers, confusion showing deep within his irises.

"Tell me," she breathed, her voice filled with the hunger that he felt.

So he began, he began ten years ago when he saw the body of a dead man and heard the thunder of gunfire. He told her about the darkness and the light, about Ethan Samson and Archangel.

"Archangel…" Sadie knew the name, the myth. A woman who slaughtered the guilty and protected the innocent. To the Witness she was something else, more than just a woman or a vigilante. She was his savior.

Nine Years Ago

"The Witness shall take the stand," the Judge's voice rang through the courtroom.

He placed his hand on the Bible, swearing to speak only the truth and he did. His dark eyes locked onto those with the man being charged with murder: Ethan Samson. He described the shredded body, the sparkling glass and the trail of blood. His testimony matched that of several others and Detective Jessica

Cohen's own account of what had happened. For the briefest of instants, the Witness felt like he had done something good. He looked over Ethan Samson's head to see his own wife and daughter. Expressions of pride and terror unified them, and, for the first time, the Witness saw just how much his daughter resembled his wife.

Now

"Julia," he whispered, his eyes filled with regret, cool and clear, streaming down his face. Unlike the black rain, his tears were clear...almost pure. "My wife's name...she didn't want to have her daughter named after her..."

Sadie reached out and took his hand, it quavered beneath her touch. She had no words of consolation or grief. Nothing would ease the pain within him, and nothing could change her lack of response. They simply sat in silence while tears stained the menu that he had been hiding within. Her own thoughts felt the loss he had just uttered, filled with the same pain...

One stark sneer greeted Sadie as she helped her aging mother from the hospital. She had refused the treatment. The woman had heard the conversation, the rejection. She demanded answers, "Why didn't you two get cured?"

No words could answer her Question, the woman tried to drag them both back to the hospital. Sadie's mother pleaded with the woman until finally, through either annoyance or rage, the woman backhanded Sadie's mother. She fell, her heart as broken as her will. Sadie screamed, as she was dragged back to the place that had killed her family.

She saw the smiling face of the future president, one sterling silver needle upraised holding the cure that kills as much as the disease.

"You don't have to continue," she said, her words as kind as they were hoarse.

"I've run as far as I can," he answered. "The only thing left to do is continue."

Eight Years Ago

"You the Witness?" he was all smiles, his bright green polo practically glowing beneath the yellow sun. For once the thick shroud that had hovered over New Coast had parted, revealing a golden orb of warmth. The Witness sat on a bench, facing the store his wife and daughter had just gone into.

He shrugged, "One of them."

He would have given anything to have taken those words back. Instead all he saw was the flash of a silver knife, he heard screaming. Rising, the Witness tried to push past the man, he caught a glimpse of blood and bodies. The knife pierced his side, and he fell, the man in the polo whispering, "Ethan Samson doesn't need your sorry ass slandering his name."

The Witness found himself dying on the ground, listening to screams, his wife begging for him. He thought he was going to die, then she appeared. A shadow, a silhouette wreathed in light. She stood over him like a guardian angel, as he fell unconscious.

When he woke up, he found out that his wife and daughter had been killed, their murderers found strung up to lighting posts by their legs. As for Ethan Samson, he denied everything as he ran for presidency.

Now

"Do you think," Sadie swallowed the bitter taste in her own mouth. "That he was behind your family's murder?"

The Witness's voice grew quieter now, the weight of his past crushing his words, "He sacrificed the lives of three million people when he cured the Scythe virus. What was three more to take control of the country?"

Words were a powerful force when used correctly, but Sadie doubted anything the Witness told her would topple President Samson from his throne. Outside, wind rattled the windows of the diner and black smog turned the colorless day into the abyssal night.

"What do you think a human life is worth, miss…" The Witness began.

"Walker, Sadie Walker," she couldn't tear her eyes away from the darkness outside. "What's yours?"

"I don't have one, my name died with my family," the Witness stood and walked to the windows, Sadie found herself drawn with him, moving with him to gaze at the swirling clouds as they sailed through the city. "What do you think a life is worth, Miss Walker?"

"More than this," Sadie answered.

With that, she lost herself in the ripples and eddies of the darkness around her, and the shadows struggling within.

Ω

She woke up to the grey light of the clouded sky shining across her face. She remembered making the trek back to her apartment through the blackened streets after the storm had subsided. She could see her ruined clothes in the trash across the room, ruined by the black rain. Changing into the only remaining set of clothes she had, she was faced again with the blank page on her desk, the Question burning through her brain. *What is a life worth?*

She knew what James would say if he was there. Her brother was different than most people she had known. His unbridled optimism was entirely inappropriate for the world around him. Sometimes she couldn't decide whether the world did not deserve him or he did not deserve it. He would have told her to get off her ass and find out.

Ω

There was a jeweled line once; golden absolutes that had been undisputed. The world was either all good or all evil. No silver tongue caressed the dark greys that pervaded reality, not until Ethan

Samson. He married lies and truth in such a way that gave the nation exactly what it wanted: hope. Sadie stood in front of his engine for that hope: Fusion Incorporated. The infamous building whose crown jewel was a billboard glorified by the image of the President himself.

Glass doors led to sanitized hallways emblazoned with the logo of the company. A crimson rug burned a road to the curved reception desk that served as the dam against the tides of individuals searching for solace from the world outside. A blind-eyed receptionist greeted Sadie with a blissful smile of ignorance and asked, "What can I help you with, Miss?"

"The New Coast murders," Sadie answered, her voice curt.

Empty eyes blinked in confusion, "I'm sorry?"

"You heard me."

After the briefest of encounters with the screen, the receptionist gave Sadie an apologetic smile and told her that there was no such event. According to all files, no one had been murdered in New Coast since the anarchy after the floods. Sadie didn't need to inform the receptionist that they were pouring bullshit from their mouth. She could see the cold suspicion in the receptionist's eyes—that had been incapable of displaying any emotion just moments ago.

Giving the receptionist a golden smile, Sadie left the building feeling sick. The thick air outside only served to choke her. Her footsteps swept her to the same diner she had met the Witness in. No black rain descended from the sky as Sadie entered the diner, but she still felt as if sludge was falling down her shoulders. She noticed that where the Witness had once sat, a man in a suit now made himself comfortable.

She did her best to ignore him, instead decimating her pockets in search of money.

"Need change?" The suited man asked, looking at her. She shook her head in response, barely whispering a negative answer to his offer. He continued to watch her for a moment then took a breath, "We all need change eventually. A lot of people would love to progress but remain the same; they are always afraid of what might happen."

It took every ounce of strength in Sadie to prevent herself from running out of the diner, "Sometimes people are afraid because what they've seen."

"Seeing things is a dangerous thing," the man stood, brushing by her as he made for the door. "It gets people killed."

Urged to follow but afraid of discovery, Sadie started after the man. It was her sudden movement that saved her life; the bullet, meant for her heart, hit her shoulder instead.

She sat on the tile floor, and looked at the hole in the glass, blood running down her body. She felt numb, her limbs cold, thunder ringing in her ears. The world around her faded in and out of view. Her eyes were drawn to the hole in the glass, webs of cracks branching out from the hole. Shadows rose around her, words whispered through her ears. Someone pulled her to her feet, something pressed against her shoulder. Searing pain brought sharp colors back into her vision and sonic screams shattered her eardrums as her hearing returned to her.

"Run," was the one word she could make out. Whirling desperately, she saw a mask, a face of determination pressed something into her hands and Archangel… A woman dressed in darkness with shadows as her cape, once again said, "Run."

Sadie bolted out of the diner, holding whatever the vigilante had pressed into her hands. She ran away from the diner, losing herself among the labyrinth of buildings between it and her apartment. What she discovered there was a violation of her sanctuary. The door had been forced open and everything was strewn across the floor. Papers were shredded and furniture destroyed.

Taking a calm breath, Sadie forced herself to ignore the constant spear of pain that impaled her every time she moved her shoulder. She looked at what Archangel had given her. It was a single file, marked with the symbol of the New Coast police. She spread the file out against the table that had somehow survived the massacre unscathed. Inside the file she was greeted with hastily scribbled words: *Samson Incident Report- Detective Jessica Cohen.*

Behind that paper, she found the answers the Witness had searched for his entire life. What struck Sadie the most, wasn't the detective's report, but the photograph that came with it. She saw the bodies, and the woman she assumed to be Jessica the woman who had just saved her life.

She collapsed against the wall staring at the chaos around her. Whatever adrenaline had coursed through her, fueling courage over cowardice, determination over fear - it began to fade away and she understood what the bullet hole in her shoulder meant. Her hands shook and she whispered to herself, "What the fuck... have I done?"

She could have screamed or wailed to the deaf ears of god, but why? Nothing divine could change what had happened. Instead she reached into her pockets and withdrew a wallet, visualizing the suited man brushing against her. Flipping through it, she found a small piece of paper containing an address scrawled hastily against the paper. Standing brought waves of pain back to her, but Sadie only gritted her teeth and ignored the piercing whispers drawing her towards submission.

The building overlooked the diner, a perfect spot to fire a fatal bullet. Sadie ascended the stairs towards the apartment listed on the paper. The only light streamed through greasy windows coated with dust, illuminating a golden symbol: S2, the number of her destination. She reached out to touch the dark brown surface when a breath of fate caused the door to slide open slightly. Pushing it open caused a clamor of insanity, footsteps scrambling for shadows.

Sadie was greeted with the barrel of a gun, and as she gazed into its dark void, she noticed it was shaking.

"St..stay away…" a weak voice pleaded. "I…I'll sh…shoot!"

Darkly, Sadie pushed her jacket from her shoulder to reveal the bandages, "You already did."

Looking into the man's fearful eyes, she saw the recognition, and he dropped the gun, "Oh god…I…please you don't understand…d…don't kill me…p...please.!"

He'd stayed in the exact spot he'd shot her from, she could see the open window and the rifle on the ground. Hate washed over her eyes, and she pushed him backwards, grabbing his gun and aiming at his head.

"You tried to kill me, what did you do to the Witness?" she growled, her voice feral.

"He's dead…" the man wept.

She was tempted to pull the trigger, all she wanted was to put a bullet in his head, wasn't it justice? An eye for an eye, a heart for a heart, three million for a world, balancing the scales with one piece of lead. Instead she asked, "WHY?"

"I COULDN'T TAKE IT!" he screamed. "He was talking about the president! Spreading lies! And you were there…you're James Walker's sister, he's a damn journalist for crying out loud! Imagine what that media dog would have done!"

"So you killed him because of something I might do?"

"I killed him because President Samson saved my life! He saved me and this man was going to destroy him!"

"You had Scythe?" tears streamed down the man's face, one hand upraised in a pathetic attempt to muzzle the very weapon he'd once wielded.

Eight Years Ago

The President' face was bathed with the light of the warm sun, no sweat streamed down his skin as it did others. The crowd around him strained to follow the newly elected President as he walked down the street towards the center where he would be giving a speech. The man followed the crowd, trying to break through the walls of people attempting to garner any form of recognition from the president.

Shots rang out and screams broke out around him. A man in a green polo shirt broke through the crowds and roared, "GET OUT OF THE WAY!"

The gun lit up, a flash seared itself into his eyes. When the flash faded, he saw the president on the ground, blood staining his white suit. Secret Service men were dragging off the green polo clad man—then he, the future murderer, ran to the President's side.

"Why?" The future murderer asked.

"I took an oath," Ethan Samson answered, cracking a pained smile.

Now

Sadie sat in the ruins of her apartment, staring at a blank page, faced once again with the Question.

She could still see the police rushing into the building, the murderer sitting in a pool of his own tears, the empty gun near the window. They'd find the Witness's body eventually, undoubtedly the murderer would explain what had happened. Sadie found herself asking a different question: why hadn't she pulled the trigger?

Picking up a pen from the ground she wrote the Question on the paper, the first words ever to mar the plain of blank ideas. *What is a life worth?* For a brief moment a smile graced her lips, and she knew why she did not pull the trigger. For the first time in her life, Sadie felt the warmth of the sun through the grey clouds, she felt hope.

What is a life worth?

About the English Club

California State University Channel Islands Student Organization

The English Club's mission is to cultivate a vibrant community of Writers, Readers, and Educators while also providing resources for future Career Paths. English Club offers a safe space for readers and writers to prosper and grow through shared resources and support.

About the Authors

The dedicated authors published in the English Club Creative Writing Journal Volume 1 are undergraduate students at California State University Channel Islands. Each piece was written during the 2017-18 academic school year with the support of peers from the English Club. In addition, the ECCWJ Volume 1 is a CSUCI student run publication.

Made in the USA
San Bernardino, CA
27 August 2017